Inspirational Poems FROM THE Heart

Inspirational
Poems
FROM THE
Heart

FAI YEE THOO

PARTRIDGE

To order additional copies of this book, contact
Toll Free 800 101 2657 (Singapore)
Toll Free 1 800 81 7340 (Malaysia)
orders.singapore@partridgepublishing.com

www.partridgepublishing.com/singapore

Contents

Dedication

I would love to dedicate the poems to my family especially to Jojo and Peter, Grace and Donway, Tzetze and Andrew.

FAI YEE THOO

The Hero

Did we toil that hard to protest in the streets?
How worthy are we to claim for so much,
If we hadn't been diligent enough for work to be done.
Blessed are those who had helped to build the nation.

He who had silently worked for the success of the nation,
Would be honoured and inscribed on statues.
He stands tall even after his demise.
And as the years pass by his remembrance would be the bird's poo,
Upon the statue's head as not many could be
bothered who he was and what he did.
As many would be keen to be glued to their smart phone,
Than to know that He was Abraham Lincoln or Julius Caesar!

Fai Yee Thoo

The Wind

Oh wind that blows throughout the day.
Where did you get your monstrous strength?
You can be timid to give us a slight breeze.
Leaves swaying and rustling to give us a soothing sound.
Oh wind, how many miles have you travelled?
We humans fear you if you relentlessly
blow and topple the big ships.
You have character like humans..this world
would be helpless without you.
We thank you for your mighty work!

Bible..the wind blows where it wishes and you hear the
sound of it but can't tell where it comes from and where
it goes so is everyone who is born of the spirit.

FAI YEE THOO

The Desert

When light descends upon the desert floor,
The undulating sand dunes gleam with delight.
Another day has arrived, beckoning to travellers to ride,
Across the vast stretch of desert floor.
My beauty will be forever remembered as men thirst for oasis,
Fine prunes and unquenchable thirsty drinks.
The men's honour and victory would be their camels,
trampling upon the fine sand and bringing
along riches of every nation.
Camels dear, without thee, how could men travel far and wide,
Across such hot scorching sandy desert?
Your tough and padded special feet made by God,
Had made them possible for us to travel far and wide.
We thank you camels as ship of the desert,
To travel across the gleaming wondrous sand by day and by night.
The brightly lit stars with a solitary light of the moon
that would follow us wherever and whenever we travel by night.
This amazing world wouldn't have been
created just without You God!
Warriors, fighters and so called great leaders would
have passed and fought merciless victories.
You men are living on borrowed time on Planet Earth.
If the vast desert could speak to you, it would say,
"What's there to fight...Planet Earth belongs to God."

FAI YEE THOO

If I Could Be

If I could be like that small bird, that flies
around, fluttering its wings,
I wouldn't need to think of fast planes or sporty cars to tour around.

My world would be the lovely fruits and the fragrant
flowers that could satiate my appetite.
My world would be the gardens that I could
fly to my loving wife awaiting for me.
Edible fruits for the birdies awaiting for
mum or dad with their beaks ajar.
Our restfulness would be to have our wings
folded snugly for the wintry nights,
Not to be perturbed by an icy frosty night.
We are innocent of diseases and only
know when predators attack us.
We needn't be worried of accumulating wealth,
As what lies in front of us that nature provides
is abundant wealth of delectable food.

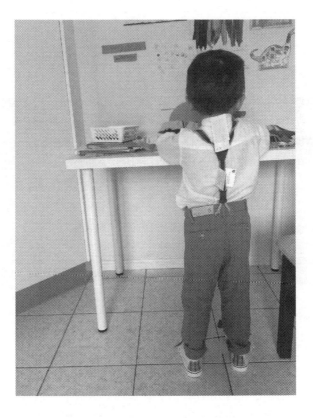

FAI YEE THOO

My Grandson Lawrence

Lawrence little hands hold on to the hands of people he loves.
Come on little man, your hands are so gentle and small
That can melt the heart of man
Lift up the spirit of people who could carry you
Lawrence dear, you are fondly missed by grandma,
Who can hold on your little hand.
Walking side by side with you.

FAI YEE THOO

Yellow Butterfly

Hi Yellow Butterfly, when were you born?
Yellow butterfly with your angelic wings, you fly so freely,
Flying high, flying low foraging for the fragrant flowers.
The daisies are dancing wildly to greet you;
the orchids and roses likewise.
They are beckoning to you to land on their
lovely petals; their buds ever blooming.
Yellow butterfly so perfectly created and pure,
You have given so much beauty around; making
everyday more glorious with you frolicking around.
Yellow butterfly fly freely.

FAI YEE THOO

The Fishermen

We love the salty sea that smiles or scorns at us.
We travel in the rickety boats far and wide not worrying much.
We have been fishing with our friends and dad
for ages; we know the tricks of the trade.
We have seen grey sky, met wind blowing relentless
and huge waves that could toss us overboard.
We being brave fishermen have been toiling to get our catch.
It's in our blood, feeling very adventurous and
we have been browned by the sun.
We know the days or time when the tide is high or low.
Nothing would make us more satisfied,
Than having the freedom to be out in the
sea and yet bring back the catch.

Fai Yee Thoo

Stanthorpe (Queensland)

Staying in a remote cottage at Stanthorpe
We had to light the firewood at a fireplace to keep us warm.
We saw the apple orchards; we tasted the richest apple pie at a cafe.
The place outside was windy, cloudy and icy cold,
All we had wanted was hot chocolate and
warm coffee to satiate our coldness.
The best chocolate drink was served and the
varied chocolates were sold there too.
Stanthorpe is proud of its rocky belt that stretches far and wide.
You can meet the Kangaroos hopping around with
joeys crawling out from the mums' pouches!
Looks like they would want to ask us, why do you come around?
Hoping to catch hold of the baby kangaroos
and to give them a big hug!
We love you and we shouldn't infringe into your sanctuary!

FAI YEE THOO

The Smoker

If I can't get my puff,
"Sir, are you going to England?"
"Yes of course but mind you the journey is 16 hours!"
Dubai was my first transit.
I searched and searched for a puff.
There wasn't an open place for a puff.
Alas I found a den full of smokers, Covered
with smoke, I needn't light a cigarette!
A cool smoker like myself can only find solace
smoking in a comfortable zone.
Not in any darn place with Eyes staring at me.
London I did arrive.
Nothing surprised me more than to enjoy
my puff and a a cup of coffee.

FAI YEE THOO

The Mighty Eagle

It's Winter and the air is icy cold,
Yonder soars an eagle with a wingspan of 4 feet across;
Carefree but immensely focussing on its prey.
A vastness of forests with its varied myriad of
colours being painted right before my eyes.
It circles and flies around looking for its food,
Poor creatures of the forest; if you can see
another morning, you had survived!

FAI YEE THOO

The Sun

Who are you? What are you made of?
You stand there burning forever and forever.
You are so strong to pull us round and round.
We being in the planetary belt have been
mesmerised by your immense strength!
How long will you be there to give us the twirl?
We being merry, love to twirl by ourselves.
We adore you, our fatherly sun!

FAI YEE THOO

The Stray Black Cat

Hi skinny stray black cat,
Why are you going away?
Haven't you caught anything or been fed?
Hi, you're returning to sit under the swing.
What's on your mind?
You can't sleep as your stomach is growling.
Look as though you're prowling.
Beware you birds foraging for food,
As your freedom would be gone once
you're clawed or prowled upon.
Your feathers flying everywhere; to be blown away by the wind.

FAI YEE THOO

Arthur Dear,

How old are you dearest Arthur?
I'm 5, Popo dearest,
I can swim and beat the rest when I'm the best,
I love the Ninja's as I love to jump like them!
Mum loves me most when I'm not jumping around,
You know I can eat fast if I'm not picky,
Mum loves me most when I'm not sticky!
When I'm 6 I'm even stronger than u can imagine
cos I'm Arthur the Great!

FAI YEE THOO

Love

Love is kind, love is patient, ever forgiving.
It shouldn't keep records of wrongdoings.
Humans need love too to survive well.
What is the driving force for a man to aspire to his highest?
It should be the love of the job, the love of his life.
The loving nature of mankind should always be treasured.
We shouldn't always have a revengeful spirit,
Forgive those who had harmed us and the world can be healed.
Everyone must pray and start on a clean note
for the peace and love of mankind.
Forgiveness and love heal people of every race and of any religion.
We must start today!

FAI YEE THOO

Being Fishermen

They have all the time been out in the sea.
It's in their blood, burning breathing inside their body
Nothing can match their freedom and adventure in the sea,
As they have met the most stormy sea.
Their catch of the day whether big or small,
Would not stop them from being fishermen.
It's the love of their lives!

FAI YEE THOO

Love for Mankind

This poem carries a message,
That love is very powerful as love encompasses all.
And most importantly man should be able to forgive.
We must pray and resist the evil spirit,
To entice man to kill in the most abominable way.
It's only possible if we have love for mankind.

FAI YEE THOO

Butterfly

It makes one wonder,
That such a beautiful butterfly,
Has been created in our lovely garden.
It adds live to the garden and it can help in pollination.
This butterfly is so carefree
And enjoying immensely not knowing,
When it will be gone so shortly.

Fai Yee Thoo

The Place called Stanthorpe

It's the coldest place in Queensland when it's winter.
It has fine orchards and a cafe,
That sells the best apple cider.
This place has a very special chocolate drink,
And snow had fallen here.
There's a rocky belt where the Kangaroos thrive,
And peeped around.
We stayed in an old cosy cottage,
Where we had to light the firewood in a fireplace on this cottage.

FAI YEE THOO

Smoking

The addiction to smoking is so unbearable,
After being deprived for so many hours travelling in a plane.
The smoker was earnestly searching for a place to smoke,
But he was shocked to see so many smokers,
Being crowded in a place than in places he could find
In the gardens outside that he had travelled before.

Fai Yee Thoo

The Eagle

The eagle usually flies circling around,
And with its sharp eyes focussing on its prey.
It's wings and talons are strong.
If it swoops down it has targeted on its prey.

FAI YEE THOO

Sun

It's truly God's perfect creation,
To position the world and with this miraculous sun,
Just at the perfect distance.
It gives us the magnetic pull,
And we being on Planet Earth are twirled
And we should be merry and be thankful in having the Sun

Fai Yee Thoo

Arthur

Arthur is a grandson.
He is very active, cheerful but picky on food.
Popo is what he called his grandma.
He has great strength and dreaming to be a Ninja.
He will be great one day

FAI YEE THOO

The Hero

The writer thinks that the protesters and destructive warriors,
Had not worked hard at all.
Why should they destroy?
Those who had worked diligently to build
the nation should be honoured.
We can see statues being built to honour them.
Regretfully many people of today are not bothered,
With these great leaders than to be hooked on the smart phones.

Fai Yee Thoo

The Black Cat

This stray black cat is skinny,
As it couldnt catch much food.
The writer is wondering what it would do next.
Most probably it would prowl,
On the birds that are unaware.

FAI YEE THOO

Wind

The writer is amazed and wonders,
What the wind can do miraculously.
Most of the time soothing,
But at times ruthlessly merciless,
Topling everything on its way.

FAI YEE THOO

Lawrence

A grandson to the writer.
He is so loveable and sweet.
He doesn't hold your hands,
Unless he gets along very well with you.
As we stay in different countries,
We can't be meeting too often.
You can't resist holding his small little hands,
As he is so cute and cheerful.

FAI YEE THOO

Desert

Camels had been the main beast of burden,
During the ancient and today in desert regions.
God had created them for men to travel.
Men should not be fighting as everything belongs to God
As He had claimed as quoted

Fai Yee Thoo

Life Has a Purpose

Be thankful to God that we can see, hear,
talk and walk with no disabilities.
Look around and be thankful to God that
you are not blind, mute or disabled.
Parents stop comparing the marks of your
kids with their peers or friends.
We will try our best to study and to please oneself and to our family.
Do not be frustrated or depressed when we
fail our test or exams at times.
There are so many careers or things we can be good
at if we take the trouble to learn a trade.
We don't take our lives just because we can't do well.
We should be brave to face the world and pray to God often.
Remember our parents love us dearly!
We should grow up to be a useful citizen and try
to help people who might need your help.
Live with a purpose and not be selfish to think of oneself only.
Always remember you are a family and you should never hurt them.
By committing suicide you are hurting your family.
We must be ready to face the world.

FAI YEE THOO

Different Races Can Mingle Better

How we have seen people of different races can adapt and adopt better, if they allow their children to study in a Chinese school.

Children today(non- Chinese) can mingle better if they study together with Chinese kids of the same Chinese school. Young people do not keep hatred and they are usually very innocent.

In our country, Malaysia we have around 15000 non Chinese studying in the Chinese schools. They have mastered Chinese so that they can answer the examination questions in mathematics and science. They have to answer the essay and a lot of comprehension in Chinese. They are able to read the Chinese newspapers. Most of them would study until UPSR (like primary 6 in Singapore), the primary levels are from age 7-12 here. They are healthily mixing with the Chinese and knowing better of their cultures and idiosyncrasies. If you don't look at his face you might think that he is a Chinese as he can speak Chinese so fluently. Children can master a language more fluently because of exposure and given the text to be taught well in their chosen schools.

I've been giving tuition here for years and I'm contented to find more Muslims attending Chinese tuition here. These kids are quite happy and contented talking to the Chinese teachers fluently. These children have kept well their own culture as they are good in their Malay and English too. We are a very matured and independent nation and parents are given the freedom to choose their own school. Our nation is very blessed as the children here are well versed in Arabic as many Muslims have sent their children for Arabic studies.. There are many non Chinese who had enrolled their kids to pursue their children's education in Chinese schools. We are a well prepared nation ever ready to accept and to learn more. The progress of education has been cared by our prime ministers. They had and continuously showed exemplary leadership. We have been very united because of our good leadership. Malaysia will be ever ready to do business with the people of every nation.

FAI YEE THOO

If I could be

The writer dreams that a little bird can have a more loving life,
With his wife in his comfortable nest.
They are not troubled or stressed like humans always competing,
In accumulating wealth and showing off.
They don't know of diseases as they are naturally contented,
If they can have food and freely flying around
With his loved ones, innocent about death.

FAI YEE THOO

Snowing at Mount Fuji

Mount Fuji, Mount Fuji,
Why are you always being hidden by the clouds?
We love to take a glimpse of you
As you look so tranquil, covered by the creamy white snow!
Mesmerising the Sakura flowers in full bloom,
Some being white, pinkish and dark pinkish.
My Dear, is it snowing?
Yes, it's a freak snow; snowing heavily
Onto the rooftops of houses, onto the sakura
flowers and the coniferous trees.
It's a sight to behold.
Wondrous snow falling gently on my nose and on my hair,
The air is chilly and we being silly
I look like a snowy bear!
Being frozen cold but having such a mesmerising scenery
It's like we are in Paradise!
We salute to you Mount Fuji, in Japan.

FAI YEE THOO

Mount Fuji

This is one of the loveliest landmark of Mout Fuji
As one can see it more clearly in summer than winter.
We are crazy when we experience snow falling,
Covering the whole area with a mesmerising scenery.
As it's the sakura season with flowers blooming,
Around April snowing doesn't occur.
We were so blessed to experience freak snowing for a day.
This combination of snowing onto houses.
The Sakura flowers and on the writer were unparalleled,
To any scenery the writer has ever seen

FAI YEE THOO

Kathleen's Spectacles

Where's my home?
I'd travelled from Hong Kong to Singapore.
I'm very fond of the lady who wears me,
But where is she?
I broke my arm
And had my arm fixed in her hometown.
We had a very hectic schedule in Singapore,
I'm counting the days to be with her again,
GUIDING her wherever she goes.
WE LOVE watching the cats being groomed,
Kathleen Dearest, when are you taking me home?

Printed in the United States
By Bookmasters